TRADITION. EXPERIENCE.
TRANSFORMATION.

Formatio books from InterVarsity Press follow the rich tradition of the church in the journey of spiritual formation. These books are not merely about being informed, but about being transformed by Christ and conformed to his image. Formatio stands in InterVarsity Press's evangelical publishing tradition by integrating God's Word with spiritual practice and by prompting readers to move from inward change to outward witness. InterVarsity Press uses the chambered nautilus for Formatio, a symbol of spiritual formation because of its continual spiral journey outward as it moves from its center. We believe that each of us is made with a deep desire to be in God's presence. Formatio books help us to fulfill our deepest desires and to become our true selves in light of God's grace.

A GUIDE TO MORNING AND EVENING PRAYER

ceLtic
Devotions

caLvIn mILLeR

IVP Books

An imprint of InterVarsity Press
Downers Grove, Illinois

InterVarsity Press
P.O. Box 1400, Downers Grove, IL 60515-1426
World Wide Web: www.ivpress.com
E-mail: email@ivpress.com

©2008 by Calvin Miller

InterVarsity Press® is the book-publishing division of InterVarsity Christian Fellowship/USA®, a movement of students and faculty active on campus at hundreds of universities, colleges and schools of nursing in the United States of America, and a member movement of the International Fellowship of Evangelical Students. For information about local and regional activities, write Public Relations Dept., InterVarsity Christian Fellowship/USA, 6400 Schroeder Rd., P.O. Box 7895, Madison, WI 53707-7895, or visit the IVCF website at <www.intervarsity.org>.

Unless otherwise noted, Scripture quotations are taken from the Holman Christian Standard Bible®, copyright ©1999, 2000, 2002, 2003 by Holman Bible Publishers. Used by permission.

Other permissions are listed on page 131.

Design: Cindy Kiple
Images: red background: Duncan Walker/iStockphoto
arch: Carolyn Bross/Getty Images
square scroll: Andy Dean/iStockphoto

ISBN 978-0-8308-3576-8

Printed in the United States of America ∞

Library of Congress Cataloging-in-Publication Data

Miller, Calvin.

  Celtic devotions: a guide to morning and evening prayer / Calvin Miller.
     p. cm.
  Includes bibliographical references.
  ISBN-13: 978-0-8308-3505-8 (cloth: alk. paper)
  1. Devotional calendars. 2. Celts—Prayers and devotions. I. Title.
  BV4811.M54 2007
  242'.2—dc22

                                                                                        2007038408

P	17	16	15	14	13	12	11	10	9	8	7	6	5	4	3	2	1
Y	26	25	24	23	22	21	20	19	18	17	16	15	14	13	12		

acknowledgments

Besides the host of Celtic scholars I have leaned on in the writing of this book, I would like to thank above all Seán Ó Duinn OSB, a wonderful Celtic scholar who I had the privilege of studying with during my stay at Glenstall Abbey. I know of no one who is a better scholar or confident minister than he. He not only speaks fluent Gaelic, he is from a strong Irish heritage that allows him a flawless understanding of Celtic life. In addition to all his duties at Glenstall he spent a great deal of time with me instructing both me and my Beeson colleagues in the life that centers on union with Christ. We are all much the richer for his life in our midst.

Calvin Miller

to the reader

Psalm 119 appears as a central Scripture reading throughout this entire thirty day devotional season. I have chosen to focus on this psalm because it formed the important center of Celtic praise. In Ireland it was once referred to as *The Biáit*. The word comes from Psalm 119:1, which begins *Beati immaculati in via*, "Blessed are the undefiled in the way."

Celts believed that the psalm was connected with the captivity of the Jews in Babylon. They believed that on their return from Babylon to Jerusalem these Jews recited the Psalm, moving 176 paces every day, which just happens to be the number of verses in the psalm. Seán Ó Duinn says that the daily recitation of the 176 verses of Psalm 119 over the year long journey of 365 days symbolized for Celts the journey from hell to heaven. Babylon for them was a symbol of hell, and Jerusalem the symbol of heaven.

However one envisions the centrality of the 119th Psalm, it must be seen as a Scripture for people with a very mobile lifestyle. So much of the songs and prayers included in this volume are written by a people who are on a journey. The entire tradition of the Celts is rural and in most senses very stable, but on the other hand they were a people whose monks were missionaries committed to sail the open sea and the continents beyond their isolated island world in the Hebrides. Perhaps as you read through the psalm at the center of this book you will remember that you too are a pilgrim whose pilgrimage, like that of the Celts, will only find its true destiny as a journey into the eternal presence of God.

So for the next thirty days let us travel in the company of Psalm 119. In the *Biáit* we too shall find the devotion and wisdom the Celts found as they walked the way before us.

In addition to the centrality of this psalm, I have leaned heavily on the *Carmina Gadelica*, a collection of early and traditional "Gaelic songs" collected in the late nineteenth century by Alexander Carmichael and first published in 1895. They have become the most popular source of Celtic piety and are rich with Christian devotion. Certainly no devotional work on the Celts would be thorough without them. Unless it is my own work the Celtic poetry in this volume is properly credited. May this volume lead both you and me to a deeper relationship with others and with Christ.

Calvin Miller
Birmingham, Alabama

small things

It were as easy for Jesu
To renew the withered tree
As to wither the new
Were it His will so to do.
Jesu! Jesu! Jesu!
Jesu! meet it were to praise Him.

There is no plant in the ground
But is full of His virtue,
There is no form in the strand
But is full of His blessing.
Jesu! Jesu! Jesu!
Jesu! meet it were to praise Him.

There is no life in the sea,
There is no creature in the river,

There is naught in the firmament,
But proclaims His goodness.
Jesu! Jesu! Jesu!
Jesu! meet it were to praise Him.

There is no bird on the wing,
There is no star in the sky,
There is nothing beneath the sun,
But proclaims His goodness.
Jesu! Jesu! Jesu!
Jesu! meet it were to praise Him.

CARMINA GADELICA

Christ, the incarnate Son of God, fills the natural world with his presence. The natural world came to be as he breathed into existence his ornate and richly varied realm of life. The earth spins at his command. Then, when every butterfly and blossom is in place, he makes us a present of his glorious globe; it is ours as he is ours. But the pleasure of keeping his universe a-spin is only surpassed by the joy he finds in keeping us secure. His arms wrap around the cosmos, yet his gigantic love folds us into the smaller, ornate niches of his grace. We are each of us proof that Christ loves the little things his Father formed.

MORNING READING

How happy are those whose way is blameless,
who live according to the law of the LORD!
Happy are those who keep His decrees
and seek Him with all their heart.
They do nothing wrong;
They follow His ways.

PSALM 119:1-3

MORNING PRAYER

Lord, there is no seedling in the thicket that does not call you its maker. And I, too, come knowing that whatever the quality of my life is, it is thou, O God, who stamped your purpose on my soul. So I must praise you lest the silent stones grow tongues and do what I would not. Amen

EVENING READING

The palmful of the God of Life,
The palmful of the Christ of Love,
The palmful of the Spirit of Peace,
Triune
Of grace.

CARMINA GADELICA

EVENING PRAYER

May I speak each day according to Thy justice,
Each day may I show Thy chastening, O God;
May I speak each day according to Thy wisdom,
Each day and night may I be at peace with Thee.
Each day may I count the causes of Thy mercy,
May I each day give heed to Thy laws;
Each day may I compose to Thee a song,
May I harp each day Thy praise, O God.
May I each day give love to Thee, Jesu,
Each night may I do the same;
Each day and night, dark and light,
May I laud Thy goodness to me, O God.

CARMINA GADELICA

walking the path

My walk this day with God,
My walk this day with Christ,
My walk this day with Spirit,
The Threefold all-kindly:

Ho! Ho! Ho! The Threefold all-kindly.
My shielding this day from ill,
My shielding this night from harm,
Ho! Ho! Both my soul and my body,
Be by Father, by Son, by Holy Spirit:
By Father, by Son, by Holy Spirit.

Be the Father shielding me,
Be the Son shielding me,
Be the Spirit shielding me,
As Three and as One:
Ho! Ho! Ho! As Three and as One.

CARMINA GADELICA

We walk with God "the Threefold all-kindly." As the eagle covers her young, so we rest beneath the shelter of his wings. The sun cannot smite us by day, the moon does no battle with us by night, for we are safe beneath the shielding armor of eternity. The arrows that fly but weakly strike the shields made from his promises and we, uninjured, stand to praise him. We are encased in love. We are indestructible. Eternity is our noun. Eternal is our adjective. Live! and Praise! These are our God-imperative commands.

MORNING READING

You have commanded that Your precepts be diligently kept.
If only my ways were committed to keeping Your statutes!
Then I would not be ashamed when I think about all
    Your commands.
I will praise You with a sincere heart when I learn Your
    righteous judgments.
I will keep Your statutes; never abandon me.

PSALM 119:4-8

MORNING PRAYER

Our Father,
This step I take, do you take this step too?
The way I traveled yesterday at sunny noon,
were you with me in the sunshine?

Last night—at midnight—

when the gloom was thick where I doubted.

Did you fold me in your presence?

I am always faltering, are you at my right hand?

I sit now in the shade to contemplate the desert

through which I soon shall pass.

Tell me before I feel the burning sand of my long journey.

Do you go with me?

Amen

EVENING READING

God's Aid

God to enfold me,

God to surround me,

God in my speaking,

God in my thinking.

God in my sleeping,

God in my waking,

God in my watching,

God in my hoping.

God in my life,

God in my lips,

God in my soul,

God in my heart.

God in my sufficing,

God in my slumber,

God in mine ever-living soul,

God in mine eternity.

CARMINA GADELICA

EVENING PRAYER

The path I walk, Christ walks it.
     May the land in which I am be without sorrow.
May the Trinity protect me wherever I stay, Father,
     Son, and Holy Spirit.
Bright angels walk with me—dear presence—in every
     dealing.
In every dealing I pray them that no one's poison
     may reach me.
The ninefold people of heaven of holy cloud, the
     tenth force of the stout earth.
Favourable company, they come with me, so that the
     Lord may not be angry with me.
May I arrive at every place, may I return home; may
     the way in which I spend be a way without loss.
May every path before me be smooth, man, woman
     and child welcome me.
A truly good journey! Well does the fair Lord show
     us a course, a path.

ST. COLUMBA

ecstasy of praise

June 18th, 1735, *being in secret prayer, I felt suddenly my heart melting within me like wax before the fire with love to God my Saviour; and I also felt not only love, peace, etc. but longing to be dissolved, and to be with Christ; then was a cry in my inmost soul, which I was totally unacquainted with before, Abba Father! Abba Father! I could not help calling God my Father; I knew that I was his child, and that he loved me, and heard me. My soul being filled and satiated, crying, "Tis enough, I am satisfied. Give me strength, and I will follow thee through fire and water." I could say I was happy indeed! There was in me a well of water, springing up to everlasting life, John 4:14. The love of God was shed abroad in my heart by the Holy Ghost, Romans 5:5.*

THE CONFESSION OF HOWEL HARRIS

The writings of the Celts teach us about a deep thankfulness. Blessed is God, for all his gifts. But blessed all the more is God for the ecstasy that is born in loving him. How wonderful is his joy! It overspills the edges of our self-control. Through the rapture born in worship we are filled with a generous joy that sloshes over our stability and we feel too much to keep the pressure of our praise within a formal cup. Propriety forgets itself and dances like David before the ark of God.

We weep.

We laugh.

We praise.

Delight has taken charge and loving God owns the day.

MORNING READING

How can a young man keep his way pure? By keeping Your word.

I have sought You with all my heart; don't let me wander from
    Your commands.

I have treasured Your word in my heart so that I may not sin
    against You.

LORD, may You be praised; teach me Your statutes.

With my lips I proclaim all the judgments from Your mouth.

I rejoice in the way revealed by Your decrees as much as in all riches.

I will meditate on Your precepts and think about Your ways.

I will delight in Your statutes; I will not forget Your word.

PSALM 119:9-16

MORNING PRAYER

Lord, be it thine,
Unfaltering praise of mine!
And, O pure prince! Make clear my way
To serve and pray at thy sole shrine!
Lord, be it thine,
Unfaltering praise of mine!
O father of souls that long,
Take this my song and make it thine!

O'LAOGHAIRE

EVENING READING

I would like to have the men of Heaven
In my own house:
With vats of good cheer
Laid out for them.

I would like to have the three Marys,
Their fame is so great.
I would like people
From every corner of Heaven.

I would like them to be cheerful
In their drinking,
I would like to have Jesus too

Here amongst them.

I would like a great lake of beer
For the King of Kings,
I would like to be watching Heaven's family
Drinking it through all eternity.

PEIG SAYERS

EVENING PRAYER

I am giving Thee worship with my whole life,
I am giving Thee assent with my whole power,
I am giving Thee praise with my whole tongue,
I am giving Thee honour with my whole utterance.
I am giving Thee reverence with my whole understanding,
I am giving Thee offering with my whole thought,
I am giving Thee praise with my whole fervour,
I am giving Thee humility in the blood of the Lamb.

I am giving Thee love with my whole devotion,
I am giving Thee kneeling with my whole desire,
I am giving Thee love with my whole heart,
I am giving Thee affection with my whole sense,
I am giving Thee my existence with my whole mind,
I am giving Thee my soul, O God of all gods.

CARMINA GADELICA

JOYOUS DEATH

Be each saint in heaven,
Each sainted woman in heaven,
Each angel in heaven
Stretching their arms for you,
Smoothing the way for you,
When you go thither
Over the river hard to see;
Oh when you go thither home
Over the river hard to see.

May the Father take you
In His fragrant clasp of love,
When you go across the flooding streams
And the black river of death.

The love of your Creator be with you.

Be the eye of God dwelling with you,
The foot of Christ in guidance with you,
The shower of the Spirit pouring on you,
Richly and generously.

The love and affection of the heavens be to you,
The love and affection of the saints be to you,
The love and affection of the angels be to you,
The love and affection of the sun be to you,
The love and affection of the moon be to you,
Each day and night of your lives,
To keep you from haters, to keep you from harmers,
To keep you from oppressors.

CARMINA GADELICA

Death was always at hand for the Celts, living in an era of disease, famine and war. In our prayers today we ask God to prepare us. Homecoming should not be an act of terror. *God, allow us to approach your greater light without shielding our eyes against the radiance.*

MORNING READING

My life is down in the dust; give me life through Your word.
I told You about my life, and You listened to me;
  teach me Your statutes.
Help me understand the meaning of Your precepts so that I can
  meditate on Your wonders.
I am weary from grief; strengthen me through Your word.

PSALM 119:25-28

MORNING PRAYER

Thou great God of salvation,
Pour Thy grace on my soul
As the sun of the heights
Pours its love on my body.

I must needs die,
Nor know I where or when;
If I die without Thy grace
I am thus lost everlastingly.

Death of oil and of repentance,
Death of joy and of peace;
Death of grace and of forgiveness,
Death of Heaven and life with Christ.

CARMINA GADELICA

EVENING READING

May the Father take you
In His fragrant clasp of love,
When you go across the flooding streams
And the black river of death.

May Mary Virgin's Son Himself
Be a generous lamp to you,
To guide you over

The great and awful ocean of eternity.
The compassing of the saints be upon you,
The compassing of the angels be upon you;
Oh the compassing of all the saints
And of the nine angels be upon you.

The grace of the great God be upon you,
The grace of Virgin Mary's Son be upon you,
The grace of the perfect Spirit be upon you,

Mildly and generously.

CARMINA GADELICA

EVENING PRAYER

Our Father,

If we should die before we wake, then let us go to sleep in confidence that where we wake is not as important as the keeper of our slumber. Blest be all those who have rubbed the earthly sleep out of their eyes to find their gaze was wrapped in a new light and a better world than that where they fell asleep. They slept in the gray mist of the world that couldn't own them to wake in the golden haze of a city built foursquare. Sleep-shield us, Father, till we understand that while our sleep resembles death, our longing days are short and the thrumming of the night bell will one day be replaced by the blare of trumpets in the morning.

Amen

D A Y   F I V E

BLess the chILDRen

The crown of the King is around thy head,
The diadem of the Son is around thy brow,
The might of the Spirit is in thy breast:
Thou shalt go forth and come homeward safe.

CARMINA GADELICA

The Trinity is the mother's keeper as she sends her little ones out into the world. The casting of her children into life is a separation which demands the omnipresence of God, for God must dwell with the parents who stay at home even as he goes out with the youth who leave home. "Bless every road and every journey" is every mother's invocation as she walks her children to the gates of their maturity—

The LORD bless thee, and keep thee:

The LORD make his face shine upon thee,

and be gracious unto thee:

The LORD lift up his countenance upon thee,

and give thee peace. (Numbers 6:24-26 KJV)

MORNING READING

Keep me from the way of deceit,

and graciously give me Your instruction.

I have chosen the way of truth;

I have set Your ordinances before me.

I cling to Your decrees;

LORD, do not put me to shame.

I pursue the way of your commands,

for You broaden my understanding.

PSALM 119:29-32

MORNING PRAYER

Our Father,

Lord, the world is sometimes a dragon with teeth set to devour the dreams of our children. Help our little ones go softly from our homes remembering all we taught them of your great love and expectation. They have been taught of your law, they have met your Son and touched the scars of grace—they know how much your Son paid so they might call him *brother*. They have felt the flame and sweet wind of your Pentecostal breath. They have sampled the longing love born in the heart of those who know the word *Father* and trust the word *Son* as they begin the patient waiting for the Spirit to quicken their deadness with life.

Come Creator and sculpt your image once again.
Come Son of heaven and sit with us in Emmaus.
Come Spirit and breathe Pentecost into our small
religious habits so we can worship you again.
Amen

EVENING READING

God the Father is the shield beneath which we hide our fragile souls.
He comes both generous and large to cover us when troubles rain down
   upon us.
God the Son made of his own cross a place for our hard times and the
   wood he chose now serves our wounds.
God the Spirit lives within us like structural steel with welded braces
   so the pressures from without can never crush us.
We are triple-kept by triune love, shielded by the three in one.

EVENING PRAYER

The blessings of God be to thee,
The blessings of Christ be to thee,
The blessings of Spirit be to thee,
And to thy children.

To thee and to thy children,
The peace of God be to thee,

The peace of Christ be to thee,
The peace of Spirit be to thee,
During all thy life,
All the days of thy life.

The keeping of God upon thee in every pass,
The shielding of Christ upon thee in every path,
The bathing of Spirit upon thee in every stream,
In every land and sea thou goest.

The keeping of the everlasting Father be thine
Upon His own illumined altar;
The keeping of the everlasting Father be thine
Upon His own illumined altar.

CARMINA GADELICA

BLess THis House

Bless this house O Lord I pray
Keep it safe by night and day.

HELEN TAYLOR & MAY H. BRAHE

The world affords us a house of but four rooms. One room in which we sleep, one in which we eat, one in which we bathe, one in which we sit to contemplate the purposes of eating, sleeping and bathing. This shelter of shingles and fallen trees, of bricks and fragile glass, makes us feel safe, and the safety we feel allows us to set our secure hearts on the subject of your keeping. For when life knows no safe places, the turmoil of danger keeps us from thinking of you at all. Panic cannot teach us prayers. It may make us cry the words, "God save us!" but our eyes in such a moment are not focused on the God we petition but the terror we face. So bless this house, and as your quiet peace spills over roof and walls we will sit in your presence and practice the art of loving.

MORNING READING

Teach me, LORD, the meaning of Your statutes, and I will always
   keep them.
Help me understand Your instruction, and I will obey it and follow
   it with all my heart.
Help me stay on the path of Your commands, for I take pleasure in it.
Turn my heart to Your decrees and not to material gain.
Turn my eyes from looking at what is worthless; give me life in
   Your ways.

PSALM 119:33-37

MORNING PRAYER

God shield the house.
When the hail must fall upon the roof,
bid the ice be kind.
When the snow must come upon the shingles,
bid the cold be warmer than it wants to be.
When the floods rise against the walls,
make these bricks the exorcist that drives
the water demons from the foundation.
Bid the glazing of the windows
hold the blast of northern winds at bay.

For this home is a temple and
we—this poor band of lovers all—keep
here an altar.
Here we love the great God
and find the adoration of our Lord so full
abundance spills over to the loving of each other.
This is our sanctuary—our
holy place—our citadel of hope—our
shelter from despair.

EVENING READING

God bless the house,
From site to stay,
From beam to wall,
From end to end,
From ridge to basement,
From balk to roof-tree,
From found to summit
Found and summit.

CARMINA GADELICA

EVENING PRAYER

God shield the house, the fire, the kine,
Every one who dwells herein to-night.

Shield myself and my beloved group,

Preserve us from violence and from harm;

Preserve us from foes this night,

For the sake of the Son of the Mary Mother,

In this place, and in every place wherein they dwell to-night,

On this night and on every night,

This night and every night.

CARMINA GADELICA

come i this day

Come I this day to the Father,
Come I this day to the Son,
Come I to the Holy Spirit powerful:
Come I this day with God,
Come I this day with Christ,
Come I with the Spirit of kindly balm.

God, and Spirit, and Jesus,
From the crown of my head
To the soles of my feet;
Come I with my reputation,
Come I with my testimony,
Come I to thee, Jesu;
Jesu, shelter me.

CARMINA GADELICA

This day we come to the Christ of our completion. We are incomplete
when we face dread by ourselves. Yet I am such a pilgrim as often refuses

map and compass, then travels through the canyons of demonic fear alone. When I do at last admit there is a monster in my path, my admission sets my doubts upon me and I stumble, not to rise with any strength until I say, "Come I this day to Christ." And when my enemies but hear his name, they take my trembling on themselves. And the cross where every fear was conquered falls in splintered force and all the demons die, and I stand reciting my only requiem, "Come I this day to Christ."

MORNING READING

Remember Your word to Your servant;
You have given me hope through it.
This is my comfort in my affliction:
Your promise has given me life.
The arrogant constantly ridicule me,
but I do not turn away from Your instruction.

PSALM 119:49-51

MORNING PRAYER

Our Father,
Lord, come I this day to you!
I am not a great gift to offer you
It is my coming that is my gift.
For who among us holds within themselves any worthy offering

to the God who owns the universe?
To come to you while the entire world moves away from
you, is our only gift of worth.
And so I come this day: ignore me or use me,
save me or spend me. Use me or set
me by, I am yours.
Amen

EVENING READING

God with me lying down,
God with me rising up,
God with me in each ray of light,
Nor I a ray of joy without Him,
   Nor one ray without Him.

Christ with me sleeping,
Christ with me waking,
Christ with me watching,
Every day and night,
   Each day and night.

God with me protecting,
The Lord with me directing,
The Spirit with me strengthening,
For ever and for evermore,

Ever and evermore, Amen.
   Chief of Chiefs, Amen.

CARMINA GADELICA

EVENING PRAYER

Bless to me, O God, the moon that is above me,
Bless to me, O God, the earth that is beneath me,
Bless to me, O God, my wife and my children,
And bless, O God, myself who have care of them;
   Bless to me my wife and my children,
   And bless, O God, myself who have care of them.

Bless, O God, the thing on which mine eye doth rest,
Bless, O God, the thing on which my hope doth rest,
Bless, O God, my reason and my purpose,
Bless, O bless Thou them, Thou God of life;
   Bless, O God, my reason and my purpose,
   Bless, O bless Thou them, Thou God of life.

Bless to me the bed-companion of my love,
Bless to me the handling of my hands,
Bless, O bless Thou to me, O God, the fencing of my defence,
And bless, O bless to me the angeling of my rest;
   Bless, O bless Thou to me, O God, the fencing of my defence,
   And bless, O bless to me the angeling of my rest.

CARMINA GADELICA

Lord of all nature

For every material and every element and nature that is to be seen in the world was brought together in the body in which Christ rose from the dead.

SEÁN Ó DUINN

The Celts rarely separated the Christ of theology from the poetry of "Fairest Lord Jesus." He was in their praise, the ruler of all nature. Christ doesn't just lord it over the natural world. He inhabits it. This is not to cozy up to any Eastern views that Christ is one with the elements of his world, but Jesus is related to all life that he created. It is as Saint Francis taught: the sparrows were his sisters, the sun his brother. He pervades the world so completely a butterfly may bear witness to the incarnation, and a beetle may extol the crucifixion. All creation with a single voice celebrates the creator Christ.

MORNING READING

LORD, I remember Your judgments from long ago and find comfort.

Rage seizes me because of the wicked who reject Your instruction.

Your statutes are the theme of my song during my earthly life.

I remember Your name in the night, LORD, and I keep Your law.

This is my practice: I obey Your precepts.

PSALM 119:52-56

MORNING PRAYER

Each thing I have received, from Thee it came,

Each thing for which I hope, from Thy love it will come,

Each thing I enjoy, it is of Thy bounty,

Each thing I ask, comes of Thy disposing.

CARMINA GADELICA

EVENING READING

May the three springs praise you,

Two higher than the wind and one above the earth,

May darkness and light praise you,

May the cedar and sweet fruit-tree praise you. . . .

May the birds and the bees praise you,

May the stubble and the grass praise you,

Aaron and Moses praised you,

May male and female praise you,

May the seven days and the stars praise you,

May the lower and upper air praise you,

May the books and letters praise you.

TENTH TO ELEVENTH CENTURY, EARLY MIDDLE WELSH PRAYER

EVENING PRAYER

Blessed is the God of Father Abraham, praised by the silent glory
of the sunrise.

Blessed is the God of the wily Jacob who is praised by screaming
seagulls.

Blessed is the fearsome God of Elijah, the soaring of eagles
cry his greatness.

Blessed is midnight God of Olivet who reaches through darkness
to touch his broken Son while the storms of surge and sea
roar out his perfect love.

We look at Christ and praise the sun and moon.

We reach for God and praise the desert life of Sinai.

We feel the Spirit stir within us and our hymns teach us we
are fearfully and wonderfully made.

Father, Son and Holy Spirit:

Earthquake and fire and still small voice, we praise you.

the sanctity of all life

> My heifer beloved, be not alone,
> Let thy little calf be before thee;
> See yon bramble bush a-bending,
> And bowing down with brambles.
>
> He ho-li-vó 's a vó ri ag,
> Ri ag vó, take to thy calf!
>
> Coax thy pretty one to thyself,
> Till thou sendest to the fold a herd;
> Columba's tending shall be thine behind them,
> He made this lilt for thyself.
>
> CARMINA GADELICA

To bless the beasts and children is to admit to the sanctity of all life.
So when the Celts took their esteem for their cows to the court of the
high Trinity they did not blaspheme the sanctity of life. They affirmed
it. For a heifer is the gift of God and while she lives there is sweet milk

in the morning. And when she dies she gives her very flesh to sustain the eater. All that God gives his children is blessed, and milk and beef is blessing to the body as wine and bread are substance for the soul. Never watch a sparrow fall without praising the skies she flew and the nest she held as sacred.

MORNING READING

The LORD is my portion; I have promised to keep Your words.
I have sought Your favor with all my heart; be gracious to me according
    to Your promise.
I thought about my ways and turned my steps back to Your decrees.
I hurried, not hesitating to keep Your commands.
Though the ropes of the wicked were wrapped around me, I did not
    forget Your law.

PSALM 119:57-61

MORNING PRAYER

Our Father,

I thank you for the sanctity of all creation for it makes my life full. I thank you for the chirp of crickets for they are the tuning of your violins. The thunder is your timpani. The trumpet of the swans is but your calling given to the reeds that tune the willows. And every beetle is a tiny bionic machine of tendons and microscopic muscles that you have made to make the world rich with variety and purpose. Never did the

heifer low but that the sound of her purpose in the world woke the angels to sing again their anthems to your creativity. The world is yours!
Come claim it! We wait on tiptoe to greet your coming with our ready
praise.

Amen

EVENING READING

We are your people and the sheep of your pasture.

It is you that have made us and not we ourselves.

We were born when you breathed into us the breath of life.

And when first we woke in Eden we were greeted by a symphony of
sound . . .

> the chirping crickets, the whirring beetles, the roar of tsunamis
> and quaking of aspens.

While we're not earth's only residents

We were loved and set in charge of life.

We were called to be stewards and asked to give praise to
    all that God made.

Morning had broken, and God's throne was the universe
    and we were the audience set for applause.

EVENING PRAYER

In Thy name, O Jesu Who wast crucified,
I lie down to rest;
Watch Thou me in sleep remote,
Hold Thou me in Thy one hand;
Watch Thou me in sleep remote,
Hold Thou me in Thy one hand.

Bless me, O my Christ,
Be Thou my shield protecting me,
Aid my steps in the pitful swamp,
Lead Thou me to the life eternal;
Aid my steps in the pitful swamp,
Lead Thou me to the life eternal.

Keep Thou me in the presence of God,
O good and gracious Son of the Virgin,
And fervently I pray Thy strong protection
From my lying down at dusk to my rising at day;
And fervently I pray Thy strong protection
From my lying down at dusk to my rising at day.

CARMINA GADELICA

CREATOR AND REDEEMER

But creation is not enough.
Always in the beauty, the foreshadowing of decay.
The lambs frolicking careless: so soon to be led off to slaughter.
Nature red and scarred as well as lush and green.
In the garden also:
Always the thorn.
Creation is not enough.

Almighty God, Redeemer:
The sap of life in our bones and being is Yours,
Lifting us to ecstasy.
But always in the beauty: the tang of sin, in our consciences.
The dry lichen of sins long dead, but seared upon our minds.
In the garden that is each of us, always the thorn.

GEORGE F. MACLEOD

It was hard for the Celts to pry the creator Christ from the redeeming
Christ. Nature was made by the same hands that took the nails. In a
sense they put their broken world back together because they knew that

the same God who made the world and grieved its fallen condition also redeemed it. And the Christ of Good Friday in earlier millennia—before his hands were ever bloodied—took his turn at making butterflies.

MORNING READING

I rise at midnight to thank You
for Your righteous judgments.
I am a friend to all who fear You,
to those who keep Your precepts.
LORD, the earth is filled with Your faithful love;
teach me Your statutes.

PSALM 119:62-64

MORNING PRAYER

Our Father,

Lord, when the world was without form and void did you roll the clay into shapes of life? Did you sing on that far distant Friday, when you fashioned the caterpillar, and the cobra? And Jesus, when the evening and the morning were the sixth day, and your new and naked brothers and sisters stood strong and full of hope, did you look down at your clay-smudged hands and say, "I must wash off the earth of my creativity and clean my palms till they are ready for my finest art—my dying"? Amen

EVENING READING

A hundred welcomes to Thee, O Blessed Body,
A hundred welcomes to Thy Body that was crucified.
A hundred welcomes to Thy Body, O Lord.
O Son of God, to Thee all hail,
O Tree, whose blossoms never fail,
Thy Boughs of luck perfume the gale
As Mark and Matthew both have told us.
If Thou art willing to accept us
And hold us in thy hand as precious
Mercy I ask of Thee and grace
For me and for each who of Adam's race is
Whom God and the Church have bade us pray for.
Amen.

PHILIP WALDRON

EVENING PRAYER

I am lying down tonight as beseems
In the fellowship of Christ, son of the Virgin of ringlets.
In the fellowship of the gracious Father of glory,
In the fellowship of the Spirit of powerful aid.

I am lying down tonight with God,

And God tonight will lie down with me,
I will not lie down tonight with sin, nor shall
Sin nor Sin's shadow lie down with me.

I am lying down tonight with the Holy Spirit,
And the Holy Spirit this night will lie down with me,
I will lie down this night with the Three of my love,
And the Three of my love will lie down with me.

CARMINA GADELICA

makeR of marveLous woRks

Let us adore the Lord,
Maker of marvelous works,
Bright heaven with its angels,
And on earth the white-waved sea.

NINTH CENTURY IRISH

The Celts encourage us to think of God when we are held captive by the moonlight or feel the warmth of the dawn upon our face. All that is in the natural world is handmade by an all-gracious Father who creates the universe then gift-wraps it in light as a present for his children. Then his children must see him. They are all under obligation to do so. Everywhere the horizon marries the sky to earth, they must behold him. There, too, they must see the Son and celebrate his redemption. And so let us permit the mystery of the Spirit to possess us with that love that will not let us go. Let us relish the captivity of God and adore the bright dungeons of his grace.

MORNING READING

LORD, You have treated Your servant well,
just as You promised.
Teach me good judgment and discernment,
for I rely on Your commands.
Before I was afflicted I went astray,
but now I keep Your word.
You are good, and You do what is good;
teach me Your statutes.

PSALM 119:65-68

MORNING PRAYER

Almighty God, Creator:
The morning is Yours, rising into fullness.
The summer is Yours, dipping into autumn.
Eternity is Yours, dipping into time.
The vibrant grasses, the scent of flowers,
the lichen on the rocks,
the tang of sea-weed.
All are Yours.
Gladly we live in this garden of Your creating.

GEORGE F. MACLEOD

EVENING READING

The edge—thin places of God's Gaelic earth
Leak Christ by starlight when the mirror sea
Holds up to heaven the Holy Spirit's birth
And begs time bleed its red eternity.
Are there nail prints in the grieving hands
Of God and are there wounds on sympathetic trees?
Do the purging streams wash through the lands?
Is every hill a photograph of Calvary?

EVENING PRAYER

Behold the Lightener of the stars
On the crest of the clouds,
And the choralists of the sky
Lauding Him.

Coming down with acclaim
From the Father above,
Harp and Lyre of song
Sounding to Him.

Christ, Thou refuge of my love,
Why should not I raise Thy fame!
Angels and saints melodious

Singing to Thee.
Thou Son of the Mary of graces,
Of exceeding white purity of beauty,
Joy were it to me to be in the fields
Of Thy riches.

O Christ my beloved,
O Christ of the Holy Blood,
By day and by night
I praise Thee.

CARMINA GADELICA

protection

A Rock thou art at sea,
A fortress thou art on land,
Michael's shield is about thee,
Christ's shelter is over thee.

CARMINA GADELICA

The prayer above is the most famous of all the Loricae. The Lorica is the breastplate, that part of the shield that our brother Paul tells us to put on to protect ourselves against all the fiery darts of the wicked one. And the darts do fly. We have but two obligations, "to believe in the threeness and confess the oneness" and if we so believe and so confess we shall rise each day in power's strength.

We are encompassed in his protection. He is above us, beneath us and on every side. But best of all through his Spirit he is within us. We are overlaid and indwelt.

MORNING READING

The arrogant have smeared me with lies, but I obey Your precepts with
    all my heart.

Their hearts are hard and insensitive, but I delight in Your instruction.

It was good for me to be afflicted so that I could learn Your statutes.

Instruction from Your lips is better for me than thousands of gold and
    silver pieces.

Your hands made me and formed me; give me understanding so that
    I can learn Your commands.

Those who fear You will see me and rejoice, for I put my hope in Your word.

PSALM 119:69-74

MORNING PRAYER

The Breastplate of St. Patrick

May Christ protect me today:

    against poison and burning,

    against drowning and wounding,

    so that I may have abundant reward;

    Christ with me, Christ before me, Christ behind me;

    Christ within me, Christ beneath me, Christ above me;

    Christ to right of me, Christ to left of me;

    Christ in my lying, Christ in my sitting, Christ in my rising;

    Christ in the heart of all who think of me,

Christ on the tongue of all who speak to me,

Christ in the eye of all who see me,

Christ in ear of all who hear me.

I rise today:

in power's strength, invoking the Trinity,

believing in threeness,

confessing the oneness,

of Creation's Creator.

For to the Lord belongs salvation,

and to the Lord belongs salvation

and to Christ belongs salvation.

May your salvation, Lord, be with us always.

EVENING READING

I lie down this night with God,

And God will lie down with me;

I lie down this night with Christ,

And Christ will lie down with me;

I lie down this night with the Spirit,

And the Spirit will lie down with me;

God and Christ and the Spirit

Be lying down with me.

CARMINA GADELICA

EVENING PRAYER

Be the eye of God betwixt me and each eye,
The purpose of God betwixt me and each purpose,
The hand of God betwixt me and each hand,
The shield of God betwixt me and each shield,
The desire of God betwixt me and each desire,
The bridle of God betwixt me and each bridle,
    And no mouth can curse me.

Be the pain of Christ betwixt me and each pain,
The love of Christ betwixt me and each love,
The dearness of Christ betwixt me and each dearness,
The kindness of Christ betwixt me and each kindness,
The wish of Christ betwixt me and each wish,
The will of Christ betwixt me and each will,
    And no venom can wound me.

Be the mighty of Christ betwixt me and each might,
The right of Christ betwixt me and each right,
The flowing of Spirit betwixt me and each flowing,
The laving of Spirit betwixt me and each laving,
The bathing of Spirit betwixt me and each bathing,
    And no ill thing can touch me.

CARMINA GADELICA

confession

My *thought it is a wanton ranger,*
It skips away;
I fear 'twill bring my soul in danger
On Judgment Day...

EARLY IRISH POEM

We confess to the Lord, despite the fact that we know he will forgive us, for he did his forgiving back when Caesar ruled and executioners had hammers that were crass and killing cruel. We confess not so he will know our sins, for he already knows. But we confess so that being honest will open up our hearts and make us free. And there will be no shadows on our sunlit souls throughout eternity.

MORNING READING

I know, LORD, that Your judgments are just and that You have
    afflicted me fairly.
May Your faithful love comfort me, as You promised Your servant.

May Your compassion come to me so that I may live, for Your
    instruction is my delight.
Let the arrogant be put to shame for slandering me with lies;
    I will meditate on Your precepts.
Let those who fear You, those who know Your decrees, turn to me.
May my heart be blameless regarding Your statutes so that I will
    not be put to shame.

PSALM 119:75-80

MORNING PRAYER

There will be joy among the angels of heaven
That I am laved in the pool of confession.

O my soul, be joyful,
God is willing to be reconciled to thee,
Seize His hand while it is stretched out
To announce to thee a loving reconcilement.

Refuse not Thy hand to me, O my God,
Refuse not Thy hand, O Lord of lords,
For the sake of my Saviour Jesus Christ,
Let me not go to death everlasting.

CARMINA GADELICA

EVENING READING

Here is a friend who deserves to be loved
And praised more than any one;
He redeemed our lives, paid our debt
And cleansed us with his own blood:
Brothers come, rejoice,
Thank him, never be silent.

This is the gentle friend who remembered us
And loved us before the world existed;
This is the Lamb who came from heaven,
And bought us in such a costly way:
As long as we live, it is our duty
To remember the pure love of the Son of God.

PLYGAIN CAROL

EVENING PRAYER

Our Father,
I choose to come clean
So that all that might
Stay hidden,
Shall not in its skulking hiddenness come between us.
For I must walk with you or die.

Therefore I must confess, or sleep in guilt.

And if my sin, bled dark your

    Calvary,

May your gold Pietá of suffering

Regild my destiny.

I do confess. And I'm cleansed. Therefore I'm free.

Amen

DYING WITH CHRIST

Be this soul on Thine own arm, O Christ,
Thou King of the City of Heaven,
And since Thine it was, O Christ, to buy the soul,
At the time of the balancing of the beam,
At the time of the bringing of judgment,
Be it now on Thine own right hand,
Oh! On Thine own right hand.

CARMINA GADELICA

Dying is a time for changing worlds. A time when the heart forgets its beating. And the lungs fail to remember their dull exchange of air. Wanting company on this journey, the Celts called for the angel Michael to come to meet them at the time of dying. In his company they hold a better hand and breathe a brighter air as they approach the Lord.

MORNING READING

I long for Your salvation;

I put my hope in Your word.

My eyes grow weary looking for what You have promised;

I ask, "When will You comfort me?"

Though I have become like a wineskin dried by smoke,

I do not forget Your statutes.

How many days must Your servant wait?

When will You execute judgment on my persecutors?

PSALM 119:81-84

MORNING PRAYER

Jesus, Thou Son of Mary, I call on Thy name,

And on the name of John the apostle beloved,

And on the names of all the saints in the red domain,

To shield me in the battle to come,

   To shield me in the battle to come.

When the mouth shall be closed,

When the eye shall be shut,

When the breath shall cease to rattle,

When the heart shall cease to throb,

   When the heart shall cease to throb.

When the Judge shall take the throne,

And when the cause is fully pleaded,

O Jesu, Son of Mary, shield Thou my soul,

O Michael fair, acknowledge my departure.

O Jesu, Son of Mary, shield Thou my soul!

O Michael fair, receive my departure!

CARMINA GADELICA

EVENING READING

Dear Father, dear Son, dear Spirit,

The clock hands spin the dial at a maddening pace. The sun rises on the garden dial and the shadows of the stylus fall too spinning fast upon the Roman numerals that number my brief hours. My life is but a vapor that appears and then vanishes away. It is nothing more than the flight of a weaver's shuttle. It is the hurried trip of the sun gone fast across a shallow Artic sky. But never mind, I know two words that open heaven. And I shall speak the words amid the applause of gathering angels. And when I've said the words the gates will swing and the carpet to the throne will be as scarlet as forgiveness. And the words are *kyrie eliéson.*

EVENING PRAYER

Since Thou Christ it was who didst buy the soul—
At the time of yielding the life,
At the time of pouring the sweat,
At the time of offering the clay,
At the time of shedding the blood,
At the time of balancing the beam,
At the time of severing the breath,
At the time of delivering the judgment,
Be its peace upon Thine own ingathering;
Jesus Christ Son of gentle Mary,
Be its peace upon Thine own ingathering,
O Jesus! Upon Thine own ingathering.

CARMINA GADELICA

THE VOYAGE

The Children of Israel, God taking them,
Through the Red Sea obtained a path,
They obtained the quenching of their thirst
From a rock that might not by craftsman be hewn.

Who are they on the tiller of my rudder,
Giving speed to my east bound barge?
Peter and Paul and John the beloved,
Three to whom laud and obeisance are due.

Who are the group near to my helm?
Peter and Paul and John the Baptist;
Christ is sitting on my helm,
Making guidance to the wind from the south.

To whom does tremble the voice of the wind?
To whom become tranquil strait and ocean?
To Jesus Christ, Chief of each saint,
Son of Mary, Root of victory,
Son of Mary, Root of victory.

CARMINA GADELICA

The voyage is where the voyager sets existence against tide, quake and villainy. In their tiny coracles those missionaries the Celts called peregrines were often sailless and rudderless, so that God might let his tides and storms move his servants to whatever shore he wished them to go. And the cry of the voyager was never for better weather, but only that the boat should remain intact till God, who kept them afloat, should land them where he wished them to serve their world.

MORNING READING

The arrogant have dug pits for me;
they violate Your instruction.
All Your commands are true;
people persecute me with lies—help me!
They almost ended my life on earth,
but I did not abandon Your precepts.
Give me life in accordance with Your faithful love,
and I will obey the decree You have spoken.

PSALM 119:85-88

MORNING PRAYER

Our Father, O Christ, stop the ogres—drive out all the demons that make the world so monstrous. Take fear from my journey. Make the oceans small of wave, and short for the sailing. The way I go is yours, so take the fear from my going. You are for me a refuge, an ever present help in trouble. Therefore I will not fear, though the monsters confront me in the depths of the sea. Make gentle but constant the wind that bears my soul to continents I have not seen and battles that require my sacrifice. I trust you for the journey. Give me water in the desert and a song at midnight.

Amen

EVENING READING

O angel guardian of my right hand,
Attend thou me this night,
Rescue thou me in the battling floods,
Array me in thy linen, for I am naked,
Succour me, for I am feeble and forlorn.

Steer thou my coracle in the crooked eddies,
Guide thou my step in gap and in pit,
Guard thou me in the treacherous turnings,
And save thou me from the scaith of the wicked,
Save thou me from scaith this night.

CARMINA GADELICA

E V E N I N G   P R A Y E R

Our Father,

I would sleep tonight in the knowledge that I will wake on some shore
and whether I wake in the land of angels or earthlings, I am grateful
you will be near me at the waking and I will offer praise to whatever
dawn I see: to whatever world gives me the new light and a warm sun.

Amen

ςOD of the SUN

When the Spirit makes thin the canvas we see that the universe is a creation,
   That the worker, because he is a child of God, is a person,
And we see The Christ rising from his Cross and Grave like the glory of
   The Sun in the ailing snow to light up the seventh Heaven.

GWENALLT, WELSH, TWENTIETH CENTURY

Did Christ merely rise from the dead in the morning or was he the morning that signaled to all of heaven that death is temporary? Was it the sun who came rapping at his midnight door and called him to rise, or was it his Father who rose in flaming helium who called to him saying, "Child, sleeping is now past as death is past. Fold your grave clothes, the women with the spices are already in the garden and morning is framed by fiery footprints among the twisted olive trees now shriveled in their shame." The Celts call us to expand our spiritual imaginations.

MORNING READING

LORD, Your word is forever;
it is firmly fixed in heaven.
Your faithfulness is for all generations;
You established the earth, and it stands firm.
They stand today in accordance with Your judgments,
for all things are Your servants.

PSALM 119:89-91

MORNING PRAYER

Our Father,
Lord, I felt the morning on my skin and the warm sun which touched
my flesh felt like the blush of distant light. I can see now there is gold
in your bright fire and I know the mighty force which warms the world
was formed in that great foundry, where stood almighty love and
breathed the miracle, *"Fiat Lux."* Let there be light! Somehow Lord, it
must have sounded like the rustic Baptist, who seeing you wade into
the muddy Jordan said, *"Ecce Agnus Dei."* For in our needy world the
Lamb and Light are one.
Amen

EVENING READING

Sun

The eye of the great God,
The eye of the God of glory,
The eye of the King of hosts,
The eye of the King of the living,
    Pouring upon us
        At each time and season,
    Pouring upon us
        Gently and generously.
        Glory to thee,
            Thou glorious sun.
        Glory to thee, thou sun,
            Face of the God of life.

CARMINA GADELICA

EVENING PRAYER

Father, maker of light,
    it's dark outside in the world.
Son, light unmade and eternal,
    illumine my steps lest I stumble.
Spirit, inner flame of Pentecost,
    feed your fiery tongues of inner light and
Cleanse me for praise and service.
Amen

taking arms against evil

> No serpent ever crawled so low
> He did not dream of thrones and crowns.
>
> A REQUIEM FOR LOVE

Before Christianity ever came to Ireland, the Hogmanay ritual was there. It is more than Halloween. It is an ancient fear of all people of the world. It was a way to take arms against the forces of evil. It was a way to summon all that was right and holy to displace all that was evil and vile. Evil and vile, those anagrams from hell that take what's noble in the human spirit and shred it through the grinding cogs of power and ambition and hate. But Jesus met this virtue-shredder in the deserts east of the river. Here Hogmanay became the gift of God to the human race. Here death died. Here the oracle of ambush met the hush of the great God who stops the clamor for power with a bit of scarlet wood. And there the dying Savior strikes the hide and beats the skin and says to the house of worshiping souls—

My siblings are all free!

Begone you sinister spirits.

Come out of the holiness you dogs of hell.

Strike the skin,

The evil one is not to be found.

The counselor has filled the empty souls

With nothing but himself and it is enough.

MORNING READING

If Your instruction had not been my delight, I would have died in
   my affliction.

I will never forget Your precepts, for You have given me life
   through them.

I am Yours; save me, for I have sought Your precepts.

The wicked hope to destroy me, but I contemplate Your decrees.

I have seen a limit to all perfection, but Your command is
   without limit.

PSALM 119:92-96

MORNING PRAYER

Our Father,

Lord, thou ranger of heaven, be thou at our backs!

For it is not the enemy at front that makes us fear.

The tempter rarely meets us head on!

He hides in the foliage of Eden.

He lurks in the robes of a high priest.

He wears the shield of a Roman legionnaire and
handles the hammers of execution.
Lord of Psalm 91, be thou a shield and buckler.
Master of the universe—my universe—
lay hold on the master of ambush.
Drive out the demon who wants two thrones:
the chair of the Almighty—
and the chair of my own will
which owns the center of my life.
Amen

EVENING READING

God before me, God behind me,
God above me, God below me;
I on the path or God,
God upon my track.

CARMINA GADELICA

EVENING PRAYER

May your Holy Angels, O Christ, son of the living God,
tend our sleep, our rest, our bright bed.
Let them reveal true visions to us in our sleep, O High Prince of
    the universe,
O great and mysterious King.

May no demons, no evil, no injury or terrifying dreams disturb
    our rest,
our prompt and swift repose.
May our waking, our work, and our living be holy;
our sleep, our rest, without hindrance or harm.

MAIDIN UINSEANN

DAY EIGHTEEN

focus on christ

My speech—may it praise you without flaw:

May my heart love you,

King of Heaven and of earth.

G. MURPHY

Brigit of Ireland never took her eyes off Christ. And since the Savior occupied the center of her sight, all else she saw was far out on but the thin periphery of her vision. She saw the world, all of it, as but a picture frame that gathered its four edges around the face of Christ. How amazing that such an intense stare set on our wounded Lord should produce such clarity of sight for studying all lesser things.

MORNING READING

How I love Your teaching! It is my meditation all day long.

Your command makes me wiser than my enemies, for it is always with me.

I have more insight than all my teachers because Your decrees are my
    meditation.

I understand more than the elders because I obey Your precepts.

I have kept my feet from every evil path to follow Your word.

I have not turned from Your judgments, for You Yourself have
    instructed me.

PSALM 119:97-102

MORNING PRAYER

Our Father,

Encompass me with joy, for weeping gathers all its gloom against me.

Encompass me with love, for the world's a hating place at times.

Encompass me with summer, for there is too much ice in secularity.

Encompass me with good news, for the days
    overwhelm the soul with negativity.

Encompass me with foreverness, for I am too
    temporary to have any kind of future without you.

Amen

EVENING READING

Christ, you are the lens that brings my world into focus.

I looked at the meadow and saw only you.

I faced a beggar and in his need I saw your face.

I studied a chair and saw your throne.

And at midnight when I thought I was entirely alone,

Your presence dispelled my vacant heart.

EVENING PRAYER

Dear God of Christ,

Dear Christ of God,

"Bless ourselves and our children,

Bless every one who shall come from our loins,

Bless him whose name we bear,

Bless, O God, her from whose womb we came.

Every holiness, blessing and power,

Be yielded to us every time and every hour,

In name of the Holy Threefold above,

Father, Son, and Spirit everlasting.

Be the Cross of Christ to shield us downward,

Be the Cross of Christ to shield us upward,

Be the Cross of Christ to shield us roundward."

THE BELTANE BLESSING

the family tree

And Abraham begat Isaac; and Isaac begat Jacob. . . .
and Eliud begat Eleazar; and Eleazar begat Matthan;
and Matthan begat Jacob; and Jacob begat Joseph the
husband of Mary, of whom was born Jesus.

MATTHEW 1:2, 15-16 KJV

The Celts believed that to recite the genealogy of St. Brigit was to live free of all fear. "No fire, no moon, no sun should burn them . . . no lake, no water, no sea should drown them." But there is a higher genealogy in Matthew's book of Jesus. To call out his lineage is not just a reminder that Jesus had a family tree; it calls to mind his entire incarnation. Here the DNA splits down to glory, and the messianic gene pool reminds us that we are safe—not just because we recite the genealogy of Christ but because we claim in our repetition that God became a man and this is glorious. DNA is pronounced Immanuel, *God is with us.* We are not alone! Every day that we claim the genealogy of his incarnation, he is with us . . . forever.

We shall not be killed, eternally at least.

We shall not be harried.
We shall not be wounded.
No sun shall burn us.
No sea shall drown us.
No arrow shall wound us with any wounds
that hold us out of heaven.

MORNING READING

How sweet Your word is to my taste—sweeter than honey
   to my mouth.
I gain understanding from Your precepts; therefore I hate every
   false way.
Your word is a lamp for my feet and a light on my path.
I have solemnly sworn to keep Your righteous judgments.
I am severely afflicted; LORD, give me life through Your word.

PSALM 119:103-107

MORNING PRAYER

Our Father,
Lord, my invocation and my incantation are one!
You who are the light of heaven have the most ordinary blood line.
Your family tree looks rather like my own.
I breathe "Immanuel."
And this violent earth holds no terror that I consider a threat.
Amen

EVENING READING

I lay me down tonight
In the nourishing of your word,
Father of my friend.
My soul is made strong by the meat of Scripture.
My spirit is made sweet by the drink of your spirit.
I am in love,
    with the table of grace.
For I am filled with the good things you have provided
    and nourished by the promise of your steadfastness.

EVENING PRAYER

I lay me down tonight,
through the strength of the order of cherubim,
in obedience of angels,
in the service of the archangels,
in hope of resurrection to meet with reward,
in prayers of patriarchs,
in predictions of prophets,
in preachings of apostles,
in faith of confessors,
in innocence of holy virgins,
in deeds of righteous men.

SEÁN Ó DUINN

GOD MY SHIELD

The compassing of God be on thee,
The compassing of the God of life.

The compassing of Christ be on thee,
The compassing of the Christ of love.

The compassing of Spirit be on thee,
The compassing of the Spirit of Grace.

The compassing of the Three be on thee,
The compassing of the Three preserve thee,
The compassing of the Three preserve thee.

CARMINA GADELICA

The Lorica, the shield, was a piece of armor, worn by warriors, that provided the soldier with protection. As a symbol it is as the prayer that invoked God to provide the Celt with safety and health amid the calamities of life.

MORNING READING

LORD, please accept my willing offerings of praise, and teach me
    Your judgments.

My life is constantly in danger, yet I do not forget Your instruction.

The wicked have set a trap for me, but I have not wandered from
    Your precepts.

I have Your decrees as a heritage forever; indeed, they are the joy of
    my heart.

I am resolved to obey Your statutes to the very end.

PSALM 119:108-112

MORNING PRAYER

O Lord God, destroy and root out whatever the Adversary plants in
me, that with my sins destroyed you may sow understanding and good
work in my mouth and heart; so that in act and in truth I may serve
only you and know how to fulfill the commandments of Christ and to
seek yourself. Give me memory, give me love, give me chastity, give me
faith, give me all things which you know belong to the profit of my
soul. O Lord, work good in me, and provide me with what you know
that I need. Amen

ATTRIBUTED TO COLUMBANUS, C. 543-615

EVENING READING

Be the eye of God dwelling with you,
The foot of Christ in guidance with you,
The shower of the Spirit pouring on you,
Richly and generously.
God's peace be to you,
Jesus' peace be to you,
Spirit's peace be to you
And to your children,
Oh to you and to your children,
Each day and night
Of your portion in the world.

The compassing of the King of life be yours
The compassing of loving Christ be yours,
The compassing of Holy Spirit be yours
Unto the crown of the life eternal
　　Unto the crown of the life eternal.

The guarding of the God of life be on you,
The guarding of loving Christ be on you,
The guarding of Holy Spirit be on you
Every night of your lives,
　　To aid you and enfold you
　　Each day and night of your lives.

CARMINA GADELICA

EVENING PRAYER

Our Father,
Now I lay me down to sleep.
Set your four angels at the
corners of my bed.
I pray the Lord my soul to keep.
Manacle my waywardness to the bedposts
for my heart is so prone to stray.
If I should die before I wake,
Keep me mindful that I have but a little
while to walk the planet.
I pray the Lord my soul to take.
Make me dependent on your keeping in any
world where I might awake.

DAY TWENTY ONE

the journey

Far or near the distance
Every creature needs attention.

CARMINA GADELICA

We pray on the journey, for when we travel our destination seems all important to us. We pray when we lie down to sleep, for waking again is the goal. To lie down and never wake is to die. To travel but never come to an end is to live frustrated and unfulfilled. So we sleep and journey with the three. It is the Father who sets our head on the pillow. It is the Son who lets us sleep fulfilled. It is the Spirit who wakes us to the praise of morning. And when we travel, our three companions become the sum of our journey. It is the Father who provides the path. It is the Son who is the path. It is the Spirit who is our map and compass.

MORNING READING

I hate the double-minded, but I love Your instruction.

You are my shelter and my shield; I put my hope in Your word.

Depart from me, you evil ones, so that I may obey my God's
    commands.

Sustain me as You promised, and I will live; do not let me be ashamed
    of my hope.

Sustain me so that I can be safe and be concerned with Your
    statutes continually.

PSALM 119:113-117

MORNING PRAYER

Our Father,

Help me not to fear the road that leads to your most perfect pleasure.

Bless to me the thing whereon is set my mind.

Bless to me the thing whereon is set my love.

Bless to me the thing whereon is set my hope.

May the road rise up to meet me, then may you walk that road with me.

I mind no journey kept by two, if one of them is you.

Emmaus is a pleasure where our hearts burn in the way.

Amen

EVENING READING

Bless to me, O God,
The earth beneath my foot,
Bless to me, O God,
The path whereon I go;
Bless to me, O God,
The thing of my desire;
Thou Evermore of evermore,
Bless Thou to me my rest.

Bless to me the thing
Whereon is set my mind,
Bless to me the thing
Whereon is set my love;
Bless to me the thing
Whereon is set my hope;
O Thou King of kings,
Bless Thou to me mine eye!

CARMINA GADELICA

EVENING PRAYER

Be the cross of Christ between me and the fays
That move occultly out or in,
Be the cross of Christ between me and all ill,
All ill-will, and ill-mishap.

Be the angels of heaven shielding me,
The angels of heaven this night,
Be the angels of heaven keeping me
Soul and body alike.
Be the compassing of Christ around me
From every spectre, from every evil,
From every shame that is coming harmfully
In darkness, in power to hurt.

Be the compassing of the might of Christ
Shielding me from every harm,
Be keeping me from everything ruinous
Coming destructively towards me this night.

CARMINA GADELICA

the voice of thunder

O God of the elements,
O God of the mysteries,
O God of the fountains,
    O King of kings!
    O King of kings!

CARMINA GADELICA

Thunder is the laughter of power, the sweet roar that lightning makes as it spears the clouds with jagged splendor. Lightning is God saying, "Now can you see my majesty?" Sharpen your senses till your nervous system affirms the reality that owns you.

Lord, let my limitations
Borrow from your greatness.

MORNING READING

You reject all who stray from Your statutes,

for their deceit is a lie.

You remove all the wicked on earth as if they were dross;

therefore, I love Your decrees.

I tremble in awe of You;

I fear Your judgments.

PSALM 119:118-120

MORNING PRAYER

Lord, in each

quaking storm

Let me hear you

call out to the seas,

and clear the air

with vaulting

praise.

And then I'll know

How great you are!

Amen

EVENING READING

The Father created the world by a miracle;
it is difficult to express its measure.
Letters cannot contain it, letters cannot comprehend it.
Jesus created for the hosts of Christendom,
with miracles when he came,
resurrection through his nature.

He who made the wonder of the world,
will save us, has saved us.
It is not too great a toil to praise the Trinity.

CIRCA NINTH CENTURY, OLD WELSH

EVENING PRAYER

O Lord,
In the roar of the whirlwind,
    I hear attentively the noise of your voice
    that roars to the end of heaven.
I am blinded by your lightning that snips
    the sky between horizons.
Your voice roars in thunder to the ends of heaven
And I know your omnipotence,
    for it towers above my weakness
And I'm content to trust you in the storms.

DAY TWENTY THREE

RESURRECTION

John MacRury, Tolorum, Benbecula, said: "Tradition says that there was never a Yellow Butterfly on earth until Christ came forth from death and rose up from the tomb. The true Yellow Butterfly, they say, came out of the Holy Tomb, and that Yellow Butterfly spread throughout the world. The true Yellow Butterfly was never seen among wicked men, among evil company, evil speech, evil deeds, things hateful, things shameful, things vicious.

CARMINA GADELICA

The Celts believed the yellow butterfly was a symbol of resurrection, much as current believers believe the dove is the symbol of the Spirit. Let us remember that the Celts never said the resurrection *was* a yellow butterfly but that it was a symbol, a rich symbol, for the yellow butterfly was rare and beautiful. And those who are redeemed said, as Christ said, the way to heaven is narrow and "few there be which find it" (Matthew 7:14 KJV). Those who call Christ Lord are the keepers of the symbol. For the yellow butterfly lifts its bright wings and ever moves skyward. Finally, at death, the cocoon splits, the wings unfurl and "so shall we ever be with the Lord" (I Thessalonians 4:17 KJV). Heaven is ever more than a gathering of butterflies. But it is a gathering of earthbound believers who have at last found the outrageous rapture of wings.

MORNING READING

I have done what is just and right; do not leave me to my oppressors.
Guarantee Your servant's well-being; do not let the arrogant
    oppress me.
My eyes grow weary looking for Your salvation and for Your
    righteous promise.
Deal with Your servant based on Your faithful love; teach me
    Your statutes.
I am Your servant; give me understanding so that I may know
    Your decrees.

PSALM 119:121-125

MORNING PRAYER

Hail to you, glorious Lord!
May church and chancel praise you . . .
May plain and hillside praise you,
May the three springs praise you,
Two higher than the wind and one above the earth,
May darkness and light praise you,

May the cedar and sweet fruit-tree praise you.
Abraham praised you, the founder of faith,
May life everlasting praise you,
May the birds and the bees praise you,
May the stubble and the grass praise you . . .
May all the good things created praise you,
And I too shall praise you, Lord of glory,
Hail to you, glorious Lord!

TENTH TO ELEVENTH CENTURY,
EARLY MIDDLE WELSH

EVENING READING

There are many kinds of Butterfly, but the kind we speak of is not so
plentiful. The true Yellow Butterfly is near half an inch in length, and
stouter about the body than any other kind, covered with very pretty
down or plumage, very small about the tail, more so than any other
kind under the sun. The top of his head is like a king's crown with a
fringe around it. His hue is half-way between fine gold and the white
snow of the hill. He is always seen in summer, quiet and peaceful, without heat or flurry, above the corpses of infants or of other good people.
It is a good sign to see the Yellow Butterfly upon a corpse or near a
corpse. They say that every furrow and streak in his wings and in his
head and in his body is exactly in the manner of those that were in the
sacred corpse and body of the Saviour lying in the linen shroud.

CARMINA GADELICA

EVENING PRAYER

Lord,

When it's dying time,

I shall not die,

For while I lived I crucified myself.

    And being dead to self,

     you kept my resurrection,

     in the vault of all things sealed.

We are one, you and I.

Your death has conquered mine,

Your fearlessness has left me fearless

And your life is mine forever.

Amen

sabbath rest

On the holy Sunday of thy God
Give thou thine heart to all mankind,
To thy father and thy mother loving,
Beyond any person or thing in the world.

CARMINA GADELICA

We need to learn the lessons of Egypt just as the Celts did. We can make more bricks in six days than in seven. God, when you framed the universe, you stood and marveled over all you had made until the evening and the morning were the sixth day.

Then you rested!

Why? You are Spirit. You have no tendons to grow weary, no bones that need to rest. Perhaps the only reason Spirit rests is that you built into the universe a principle design to recreate all that was first made. You said that it was good! And in that brief reflection, you let the universe lay fallow and took upon yourself a separation from your art. Great artists keep their sabbath, for creation is the six days of effort that precede the sabbath of our celebration. To lose this six-to-one proportion is to contract a busy sickness that eats our souls.

MORNING READING

You are righteous, LORD, and Your judgments are just.

The decrees You issue are righteous and altogether trustworthy.

My anger overwhelms me because my foes forget Your words.

Your word is completely pure, and Your servant loves it.

I am insignificant and despised, but I do not forget Your precepts.

Your righteousness is an everlasting righteousness, and Your
  instruction is true.

Trouble and distress have overtaken me, but Your commands
  are my delight.

Your decrees are righteous forever. Give me understanding, and
  I will live.

PSALM 119:137-144

MORNING PRAYER

Father

I will not work six days

And call my

Industry as blest,

Until I bless one sabbath

And name that

Day as rest.

Amen

EVENING READING

In the long winter night
All are engaged,
Teaching the young
Is the grey-haired sage,
The daughter at her carding,
The mother at her wheel,
While the fisher mends his net
With his needle and his reel.

CARMINA GADELICA

EVENING PRAYER

Lying on my bed in praise of honest work is my last litany of the day.
For having spoken praise I can sleep soundly in God's name.

To say your name before I sleep does not guarantee that in the morning
I shall wake in that world which held my bed. Still it matters not for
every world is yours, as I am.

BEND THE KNEE

I am bending my knee
In the eye of the Father who created me,
In the eye of the Son who purchased me,
In the eye of the Spirit who cleansed me,
In friendship and affection.
Through Thine own Anointed One, O God,
Bestow upon us fullness in our need,
Love towards God,
The affection of God,
The smile of God,
The wisdom of God.
The grace of God,
The Fear of God,
And the will of God
To do on the world of the Three,
As angels and saints
Do in heaven;

Each shade and light,
Each day and night,
Each time in kindness,
Give Thou us Thy Spirit.

CARMINA GADELICA

God was for the Celts the hush of mystery, whose tri-unity never quit being either "tri" or "unity." The paradox of the three in one for them was a delicious ascent into glory. They spent no time in trying to unravel the enigma of the Trinity. So they took God as he was: complete within the bosom of the only mystery by which this world can be explained—the only meaning by which it may be endured. And they responded to the mysterious God in worship.

MORNING READING

I call with all my heart; answer me, LORD.
I will obey Your statutes.
I call to You; save me,
and I will keep Your decrees.
I rise before dawn and cry out for help;
I put my hope in Your word.
I am awake through each watch of the night
to meditate on Your promise.

PSALM 119:145-148

MORNING PRAYER

Our Father,

We have knees in part to serve you in their bending. For to go upon bent knees is to volunteer for being shorter than our firm straight legs might make us to appear. We are after all your children, sons and daughters of the Trinity. We have you as our Father, O God. Christ is our Brother, and the Spirit makes us one with all three. And so we bend our knee that our bodies may teach our hearts to lower their self-perception, and that our legs might entreat our heads not to be too high-minded and that our lowered eyes might entreat the Spirit to teach us fully of God's call and Christ's sacrifice. For the three-in-one has included us in a great unending circle of completeness. Father, you have called us your child, your Son has called us his sibling, and the Spirit has named us his temple.

Amen

EVENING READING

I often bent my knee in prayer and
    cursed the center of my legs for all their stiffness.
I bend my head from staring at the heavens and
    find it stubborn in its willingness to face the floor.
Humility is an impish virtue.
Let it have enough reins and it will think itself god-like.
Tighten it down and it will gloat over its holiness.

Humility is a gift and desire
   but so often it comes gift-wrapped in the arrogance of its practice.
I want to be like Jesus without the necessity of saying—
   Heal my odd hypocrisy,
      Thy will be done.

EVENING PRAYER

Dear, chaste Christ,

Who can see into every heart and read every mind,

Take hold of my thoughts,

Bring my thoughts back to me,

And clasp me to yourself.

PRAYER OF AN EIGHTH-CENTURY CELTIC MONK

HEALING

I n Christ the loving,
The holy Blood of powers.
(the name and designation of the person or animal)
Closed for thee the wound,
And congealed thy blood.
As Christ bled upon the cross,
So closeth He thy wound for thee.

In the eye of the loving Father,
In the eye of the loved Son,
In the eye of the Holy Spirit,
The Triune of power.

CARMINA GADELICA

A Carpenter in Israel held the gift he later bequeathed to a cobbler in Ireland. John Cameron, a Celtic shoemaker, held a special gift that stopped blood whose loss could in no other way be stanched. Hospitals and surgeons have come quite late in history. For all the early years of faith, there was not even an aspirin. Before the rise of science, God played an omnipotent role in all healing. And in these years God gave to his special souls of faith some rare gifts, and one of those was "the checking of blood." Would God give such a gift to a cobbler? He would!

Cameron said of his gift, "A man must live near to his God before he can stop bleeding; without that he does not receive the power." And to that soul yielded unto Christ, it might be said God's gift to John Cameron was the same one earlier given to his Son. The first to hold the gift of "the checking of blood" was that carpenter who stopped the flow of blood in others that they might be saved, yet on Good Friday never stopped the flow of his own blood that we might be saved.

MORNING READING

In keeping with Your faithful love, hear my voice.

LORD, give me life, in keeping with Your justice.

Those who pursue evil plans come near;

they are far from Your instruction.

You are near, LORD, and all Your commands are true.

Long ago I learned from Your decrees that You have established them forever.

PSALM 119:149-152

MORNING PRAYER

In the eye of thee, my father, my every need
    is cared for, each drop of
    my blood is subject to your keeping.
In the eye of thee, my Christ, your blood
    was taken that mine might flow
    with better purpose.
In the eye of thee, my Spirit, I know why
    I am given life and I am as
    grateful that my blood is checked as I
    am that yours didst flow.
For well I know that without the
    shedding of blood there is
    no remission of the world's sin.

EVENING READING

Healing is the province of God.
We may beg it, but not command it.
We may seek it, but not apprehend it.
It is God's high prize to give or withhold.
It is a treasure of grace.
Kept, it blesses the sick.
Given it extends life,

Withheld it is the door to eternity.

Its quest craves health.

Its bestowal is praise set on the tongue of gratitude.

EVENING PRAYER

Bless me, O my Christ,
   Be Thou my shield protecting me,
Aid my steps in the pitful swamp,
   Lead Thou me to the life eternal;
      Aid my steps in the pitful swamp,
         Lead Thou me to the life eternal.

Keep Thou me in the presence of God,
   O good and gracious Son of the Virgin,
And fervently I pray Thy strong protection
   From my lying down at dusk to my rising at day;
      And fervently I pray Thy strong protection
         From my lying down at dusk to my rising at day.

CARMINA GADELICA

paradise regained

G od said to Adam, who still held the
half-eaten fruit, as he walked
to the front door of Eden,
"Beyond these gates
Life will be hard.
And worse, it will be temporary."

A REQUIEM FOR LOVE

It is the temporariness of life that begs us call out for rescue.

In the illicit lusts of Adam, everything was lost. But in the devoted passing of Christ was paradise regained. And so the prize of Good Friday was our gift—our gift from God the Father, that we should live and reign with him 10,000 times 10,000 years.

MORNING READING

Consider my affliction and rescue me, for I have not forgotten
Your instruction.

Defend my cause, and redeem me; give me life, as You promised.

Salvation is far from the wicked because they do not seek Your statutes.

Your compassions are many, LORD; give me life, according to
Your judgments.

PSALM 119:153-156

MORNING PRAYER

Come Thou and dwell with me,
Lord of the holy race;
Make here Thy resting-place,
Hear me, O Trinity.

That I Thy love may prove,
Teach Thou my heart and hand,
Ever at Thy command
Swiftly to move.

Like to a rotting tree,
Is this vile heart of me;
Let me Thy healing see,
Help me, O Trinity.

POEM BOOK OF THE GAEL

EVENING READING

All alone in my little cell, without the company of a single person;
precious has been the pilgrimage before going to meet death.

A hidden secluded little hut, for the forgiveness of my sins: an
upright, untroubled conscience towards holy heaven. . . .

Treading the paths of the gospel; singing psalms at every Hour; an end
of talking and long stories; constant bending of knees.

May my Creator visit me, my Lord, my King; may my spirit seek him in
the everlasting kingdom in which he is.

Let this be the end of vice in the enclosures of churches; a lovely little
cell among the graves, and I alone therein.

All alone in my little cell, all alone thus; alone I came into the world,
alone I shall go from it.

If on my own I have sinned through pride of this world, hear me wail
for it all alone, O God!

EIGHTH OR NINTH CENTURY, OLD IRISH

EVENING PRAYER

A hymn for the Praise of John the Baptist
Now rendered powerful by the rich merits, pluck out the stony hard-
ness of our hearts, make plain the rough way, and make straight the
crooked paths.
SEÁN Ó DUINN

jesus the encompasser

Jesu! Only-begotten Son and Lamb of God the Father,
Thou didst give the wine-blood of Thy body to buy me from the grave.
My Christ! My Christ! My shield, my encircler,
Each day, each night, each light, each dark;
My Christ! My Christ! My shield, my encircler,
Each day, each night, each light, each dark.

Be near me, uphold me, my treasure, my triumph,
In my lying, in my standing, in my watching, in my sleeping.
Jesu, Son of Mary! My helper, my encircler,
Jesu, Son of David! My strength everlasting;
Jesu, Son of Mary! My helper, my encircler,
Jesu, Son of David! My strength everlasting.

CARMINA GADELICA

It is the delight of the Father to hold us in his broad arms to embrace our infant understanding and to caress away our fears. We are hedged in by love, and the Father has sent his Son to complete the circle of his embrace. And everywhere we look is Christ; he is before us, behind us, beneath us and above us. The sky cannot fall upon us for he shields us. The earth cannot rise against us, for he orders the mountains to be level and rebukes the gates of the grave. To our right he is our shield, to our left, our breastplate. In the valley of the shadow, we have a rod and staff. Our prayers are his weapons, and mighty they are for the pulling down of strongholds.

MORNING READING

I praise You seven times a day for Your righteous judgments.
Abundant peace belongs to those who love Your instruction;
nothing makes them stumble.
LORD, I hope for Your salvation and carry out Your commands.
I obey your decrees and love them greatly.
I obey your precepts and decrees, for all my ways are before You.

PSALM 119:164-168

MORNING PRAYER

Jesus, encircle me with your strength that I might follow your instruction in this day. I lay my trembling soul on the breast of God, knowing I am born into a family in which the Spirit, who sired me, has raised a hedge of steel around my fragile being. God has drawn a wondrous circle around me and set me down in the middle of it. And you, my brother Christ, are the encircler, making the circle so powerful that demons stop at its circumference. Even hell draws back within those smaller boundaries drawn long ago by a Roman cross. Lord, help me feel the power of the encircling today that I might obey you. Amen

EVENING READING

Alone with none but Thee, my God,
I journey on my way;
What need I fear, when Thou art near,
O king of night and day?
More safe I am within Thy hand,
than if a host did round me stand.

My destined time is fixed by Thee,
and death doth know his hour.
Did warriors strong around me throng,
they could not stay his power;
no walls of stone can man defend
when Thou Thy messenger dost send.

My life I yield to Thy decree,
and bow to Thy control
in peaceful calm, for from Thine arm
no power can wrest my soul.
Could earthly omens e'er appal
A man that heeds the heavenly call!

The child of God can fear no ill,
His chosen dread no foe;
we leave our fate with Thee and wait
Thy bidding when we go.
Tis not from chance our comfort springs,
Thou art our trust, O king of kings.

ST. COLUMBA

EVENING PRAYER

Thou Angel of God who hast charge of me
From the dear Father of mercifulness,
The shepherding kind of the fold of the saints
To make round about me this night;

Drive from me every temptation and danger,
Surround me on the sea of unrighteousness,
And in the narrows, crooks and straits,
Keep thou my coracle, keep it always.

Be thou a bright flame before me,
Be thou a guiding star above me,
Be thou a smooth path below me,
And be a kindly shepherd behind me,
To-day, to-night, and forever.

I am tired and I a stranger,
Lead thou me to the land of angels;
For me it is time to go home
To the court of Christ, to the peace of heaven.

CARMINA GADELICA

the uncharted sea

*Once Brendan and Brigit met and Brendan
questioned her about why in some quarters
she was considered a greater saint than he was.
"Tell me," says Brigit, "is your mind constantly on God,
are you constantly aware of him?"
"Well," says Brendan, "I am generally aware of God,
but I live a very busy and dangerous life.
Often the sea is very rough and storms arise
and on these occasions I forget all about God
as I am so preoccupied by trying to keep afloat."
"That is the explanation," says Brigit,
"For since the first day I set my mind on God
I have never taken it away from him and I never will."*

SEÁN Ó DUINN

Brendan the navigator would learn in his more seasoned voyages that
the compass and rudder are less important than the eye that the pilot

keeps focused on the Savior. A plea for grace in the unmarked sea is a better cry than a cry for chart and star. The power of Christ over all demons is a chain of grace. There is no devil so brave he would go after that disciple who is fixed in the center of Christ's love.

MORNING READING

Let my cry reach you, LORD; give me understanding according to
    Your word.
Let my plea reach you; rescue me according to Your promise.
My lips pour out praise, for You teach me Your statutes.
My tongue sings about Your promise, for all Your commandments
    are righteous.

PSALM 119:169-172

MORNING PRAYER

I beseech you, Jesus, loving Saviour, to show yourself to all who
    seek you
so that we may know you and love you.
May we love you alone, desire you alone, and keep you always in
    our thoughts.
May love for you possess our hearts,
May affection for you fill our senses, so that we may love all else in you.
Jesus, King of Glory,
You know how to give greatly

And you have promised great things.

Nothing is greater than yourself.

We ask nothing else of you but yourself.

You are our life, our light, our food and our drink, our God and our all.

AN ANCIENT IRISH PRAYER

EVENING READING

We follow Christ protected from the evil darts of Satan, by the whole armor of God.

Let us dress ourselves for battle and the mirror of our arraignment must be Ephesians six. Let the apostle be our valet as he hands to us our armor.

Finally, be strong in the Lord and in his mighty power. Put on the full armor of God so that you can take your stand against the devil's schemes. For our struggle is not against flesh and blood, but against the rulers, against the authorities, against the powers of this dark world and against the spiritual forces of evil in the heavenly realms. Therefore put on the full armor of God, so that when the day of evil comes, you may be able to stand your ground, and after you have done everything to stand. Stand firm then, with the belt of truth buckled around your waist, with the breastplate of righteousness in place, and with your feet fitted with the readiness that comes from the gospel of peace.

EPHESIANS 6:10-15 NIV

EVENING PRAYER

The compassing of God and His right hand
Be upon my form and upon my frame;
The compassing of the High King and the grace of the Trinity
Be upon me abiding ever eternally,

  Be upon me abiding ever eternally.

May the compassing of the Three shield me in my means,
The compassing of the Three shield me this day,
The compassing of the Three shield me this night
From hate, from harm, from act, from ill,

  From hate, from harm, from act, from ill.

CARMINA GADELICA

the kinG incarnate

There is but one grand miracle.
It's found where mystery dares dance
Across the dream of God
And flesh is born
As Spirit ravishes dull sod.

While the spirit touches flesh a longing is born.
It is a longing to know God.
It is a longing to taste the pleasures of his reality.
It is a crying out for help.
It is a desire for holiness,
A love for his judgments,
A grand remembrance of all his requirements.

By reason of great contrast there is only one authenticating miracle. It is the incarnation. Only this miracle enables all the others. For if God could actually become a man, then all the unbelievable things Christ did take their own believable place in his wholly believable life.

MORNING READING

May Your hand be ready to help me, for I have chosen Your precepts.
I long for your salvation, Lord, and Your instruction is my delight.
Let me live, and I will praise You; may Your judgments help me.
I wander like a lost sheep; seek Your servant, for I do not forget Your
commands.

PSALM 119:173-176

MORNING PRAYER

Keep me in good means,
   Keep me in good intent,
Keep me in good estate,
   Better than I know to ask,
   Better than I know to ask.

Shepherd me this day,
   Relieve my distress. . . .

Guard for me my speech,
   Strengthen for me my love,
Illume for me the stream.

CARMINA GADELICA

EVENING READING

The Child of glory,
The Child of Mary,
Born in the stable;
    The King of all,
Who came to the wilderness
And in our stead suffered;
Happy they are counted
    Who to Him are near.

When He Himself saw
That we were in travail,
Heaven opened graciously
    Over our head;
We beheld Christ,
The Spirit of truth,
The same drew us in
    'Neath the shield of His crown.

Strengthen our hope,
Enliven our joyance,
Keep us valiant,
    Faithful and near;
O light of our lantern,

Along with the virgins,
Singing in glory
　The anthem new.

Carmina Gadelica

Evening Prayer

Grace of form,
　Grace of voice be thine;
Grace of charity,
　Grace of wisdom be thine;
Grace of beauty,
　Grace of health be thine;
Grace of sea,
　Grace of land be thine;
Grace of music,
　Grace of guidance be thine;
Grace of battle-triumph,
　Grace of victory be thine;
Grace of life,
　Grace of praise be thine;
Grace of love,
　Grace of dancing be thine;
Grace of lyre,
　Grace of harp be thine;
Grace of sense,

Grace of reason be thine;
Grace of speech,
Grace of story be thine;
Grace of peace,
Grace of God be thine.

CARMINA GADELICA

SOURCES

DAY ONE

First reading from *Carmina Gadelica*, No. 14, p. 45.

Evening reading from *Carmina Gadelica*, No. 1, p. 7.

Evening prayer from *Carmina Gadelica*, No. 19, p. 48.

DAY TWO

First reading from *Carmina Gadelica*, No. 229, p. 203.

Evening reading of "God's Aid" from *Carmina Gadelica*, Vol. 5, as quoted in *A Celtic Primer*, pp. 150-51

Evening prayer from Columba, as quoted in *Celtic Christian Spirituality*, p. 38.

DAY THREE

"The Confession of Howel Harris," as quoted in *Celtic Christian Spirituality*, p. 85.

Morning prayer from O'Laoghaire, as quoted in *Into the Depths of God*, p. 95. Twelfth-century poem taken from *The Celtic Way of Prayer*, Esther De Waal, p. 188.

Evening reading from Peig Sayers, *An Old Woman's Reflections.*

Evening prayer from *Carmina Gadelica*, Vol. 2, No. 228, pp. 202.

DAY FOUR

First reading from *Carmina Gadelica*, Vol. 3, No. 91, p. 277, as quoted
in *Celtic Christian Spirituality*, pp. 136-37.

Morning prayer from *Carmina Gadelica*, No. 342, p. 310.

Evening reading from *Carmina Gadelica*, No. 277, p. 253.

DAY FIVE

First reading from *Carmina Gadelica*, No. 279, p. 262.

Evening prayer from "The Mother's Parting Blessing," *Carmina Gadelica*, No. 292, pp. 271-72.

DAY SIX

First reading from *Bless This House*, Helen Taylor and May H. Brahe.

Evening reading from *Carmina Gadelica*, No. 45, p. 63.

Evening prayer from *Carmina Gadelica*, No. 43, p. 62.

DAY SEVEN

First reading from *Carmina Gadelica*, No. 27, p. 53.

Evening reading from *Carmina Gadelica*, No. 2, p. 36.

Evening prayer of "Rest Benediction," from *Carmina Gadelica*, Vol. 3, p.
331, as quoted in *Celtic Christian Spirituality*, pp. 140-41.

DAY EIGHT

First reading from *Where Three Streams Meet*, p. 186.

Morning prayer from *Carmina Gadelica*, No. 234, p. 207.

Evening reading from Early Middle Welsh prayer, as quoted in *Celtic
Christian Spirituality*, p. 28.

DAY NINE

First reading from *Carmina Gadelica,* No. 370, p. 341.

Evening prayer from *Carmina Gadelica,* No. 326, p. 298.

DAY TEN

First reading, "Into the garden also . . . the tang of sin," from *The Whole Earth Shall Cry Glory,* p. 8.

Evening reading from Philip Waldron, as quoted in *Religious Songs, II,* p. 359.

Evening prayer from *Carmina Gadelica,* No. 34, pp. 56-57.

DAY ELEVEN

First reading from *Celtic Christian Spirituality,* p. 30.

Morning prayer from *The Whole Earth Shall Cry Glory,* p. 8.

Evening prayer from *Carmina Gadelica,* No. 16, p. 46.

DAY TWELVE

First reading from *Carmina Gadelica,* No. 276, p. 249.

Evening reading from *Carmina Gadelica,* No. 327, p. 299.

Evening prayer from *Carmina Gadelica,* No. 233, p. 206.

DAY THIRTEEN

First reading, An Early Irish poem, as quoted in *A Celtic Primer,* p. 164.

Morning prayer from *Carmina Gadelica,* No. 296, pp. 275-76.

Evening reading from a Plygain Carol, as quoted in *A Celtic Primer,* p. 129.

DAY FOURTEEN

First reading from *Carmina Gadelica*, No. 52, p. 67.

Morning prayer from *Carmina Gadelica*, No. 49, p. 65.

Evening prayer from *Carmina Gadelica*, No. 53, p. 68.

DAY FIFTEEN

First reading from *Carmina Gadelica*, No. 120, p. 122.

Evening reading from *Carmina Gadelica*, No. 261, p. 236.

DAY SIXTEEN

"Gwenallt," quoted in *A Celtic Primer*, p. 176.

Evening reading from *Carmina Gadelica*, Vol. 3, p. 316, as quoted in *Celtic Christian Spirituality*, pp. 137-38.

DAY SEVENTEEN

First reading, *A Requiem for Love*, p. 8.

Evening reading from *Carmina Gadelica*, Vol. 3, No. 93, p. 321 as quoted in *Celtic Christian Spirituality*, p. 138.

Evening prayer from Maidin Uinseann, *The Celtic Monk* as quoted in *A Celtic Primer*, p. 45.

DAY EIGHTEEN

First reading from *Early Irish Lyrics*, p. 4.

Evening prayer: The Beltane Blessing, as quoted in *Celtic Christian Spirituality*, p. 117.

DAY NINETEEN

Evening prayer from *Where Three Streams Meet*, p. 178.

DAY TWENTY

First reading from *Carmina Gadelica,* No. 249, p. 221.

Morning prayer from *Celtic Christian Spirituality,* p. 46.

Evening reading from *Carmina Gadelica,* No. 227, pp. 254-55.

DAY TWENTY-ONE

First reading from *Carmina Gadelica,* No. 79, p. 91.

Evening reading from *Carmina Gadelica,* No. 271, p. 244.

Evening prayer from *Carmina Gadelica,* No. 297, p. 278.

DAY TWENTY-TWO

First reading from *Carmina Gadelica,* No. 301, p. 281.

Evening reading: Ninth-century Welsh poem from Ifor Williams, *The Beginnings of Welsh Poetry,* p. 102, as quoted in *Celtic Christian Spirituality,* p. 27.

DAY TWENTY-THREE

First reading from *Carmina Gadelica,* No. 354, p. 635.

Morning prayer: Early Middle Welsh poem, as quoted in *Celtic Christian Spirituality,* p. 28.

Evening reading from *Carmina Gadelica,* No. 354, p. 635.

DAY TWENTY-FOUR

First reading from *Carmina Gadelica,* No. 80, p. 91.

Evening reading from *Carmina Gadelica,* No. 109, p. 599.

DAY TWENTY-FIVE

First reading from *Carmina Gadelica,* No. 1, p. 35.

Evening prayer as quoted in *A Celtic Primer,* p. 83.

DAY TWENTY-SIX

First reading from *Carmina Gadelica,* No. 456, p. 417.

John Cameron quote from *Carmina Gadelica,* No. 455, pp. 654-55.

Evening prayer from *Carmina Gadelica,* Vol. 3, No. 94, p. 327, as quoted in *Celtic Christian Spirituality,* p. 140.

DAY TWENTY-SEVEN

First reading: "Paradise Regained," *A Requiem for Love,* p. 146.

Morning prayer from *The Poem Book of the Gael,* pp. 157-58.

Evening reading, old Irish poem from Kuno Meyer, *Ériu 2,* as quoted in *Celtic Christian Spirituality,* pp. 34-35.

Evening prayer from *The Rites of Brigid,* p. 110.

DAY TWENTY-EIGHT

First reading from *Carmina Gadelica,* No. 240, p. 212.

Evening reading: Columba, as quoted in *A Celtic Primer,* p. 141.

Evening prayer from *Carmina Gadelica,* Vol. 1, No. 56, p. 18, as quoted in *Celtic Christian Spirituality,* p. 96.

DAY TWENTY-NINE

First reading from *Where Three Streams Meet,* p. 88.

Morning prayer quoted in *A Celtic Primer,* p. 249.

Evening prayer from *Carmina Gadelica,* Vol. 3, No. 88, p. 248, as quoted in *Celtic Christian Spirituality,* p. 132.

DAY THIRTY

Morning prayer from *Carmina Gadelica,* Vol. 3, No. 86, p. 232, as quoted in *Celtic Christian Spirituality,* p. 131.

Evening reading from *Carmina Gadelica,* No. 254, p. 225.

Evening prayer from *Carmina Gadelica,* No. 272, p. 245.

bibliography

Carmichael, Alexander. *Carmina Gadelica.* N.Y.: Lindisfarne Press, 1992.

Davies, Oliver and Fiona Bowie. *Celtic Christian Spirituality.* N.Y.: The Continuum Publishing Company, 1995.

Hull, Eleanor. "Poem of Murdoch O'Daly." In *The Poem-Book of the Gael.* London: Chatto & Windus, 1913.

MacLeod, George F. *The Whole Earth Shall Cry Glory.* Glasgow: Wild Goose Publications, 1985.

Miller, Calvin. *Into the Depths of God.* Minneapolis, Minn.: Bethany House Publishers, 2000.

———. *A Requiem for Love.* Dallas: Word Publishing, 1989.

Murphy, G. *Early Irish Lyrics.* Oxford: Oxford University Press, 1956.

Ó Duinn, Seán. *The Rites of Brigid.* Dublin: The Columba Press, 2005.

———. *Where Three Streams Meet.* Dublin: The Columba Press, 2002.

O'Malley, Brendan. *A Celtic Primer.* N.Y.: Morehouse Publishing, 2002.

Sayers, Peig. *An Old Woman's Reflections,* translated by Seamus Ennis. London: Oxford University Press, 1962.

Taylor, Helen and May H. Brahe. Hymn "Bless This House." Boosey & Co., Ltd., 1927.

permissions